Herbal Antibiotics and Antivirals:

Learn Natural Herbal Treatments That Can Cure Almost All Ailments Today

Table of Contents

Introduction

Chapter 1: Herbal Medicine Basics

Chapter 2: Herbal Antibiotics and Antivirals

Chapter 3: Herbal Medicine for Injuries

Chapter 4: Herbal Remedies

Chapter 5: Benefits and Risks of Herbal Medicine

Conclusion

Introduction

I want to thank you and congratulate you for downloading the book *Herbal Antibiotics and Antivirals: Learn Natural Herbal Treatments That Can Cure Almost All Ailments Today.*

This book contains proven steps and strategies on how to become a truly expert practitioner of herbal medicine. People have been using herbs to treat their ills and ailments for thousands of years. Not only is herbal medicine all-natural and affordable, but it can also provide effective treatments for cuts, aches, and illnesses.

In fact, the benefits of herbal treatments don't even end there! Many herbs have also shown to benefit the body and the brain in other ways as well, stabilizing mood, stimulating brain function, and strengthening the immune system. Herbs contain a whole host of benefits for the entire body.

Here's an inescapable fact: you will get sick at some point in your life. Sickness and pain are natural parts of life. Whether you're bothered by the common cold or asthma, acid reflux or depression, your body and mind will be affected by the side effects of living and aging. However, all of these things and more can be treated with herbal remedies.

If you do not develop your knowledge about herbal remedies, you'll be left to suffer through sickness with countless bottles of expensive prescriptions and endless visits to the doctor's office, all to solve a problem that might have been treated—or even *prevented*—with the safe, proper use of a few natural herbs.

It's time for you to become an amazing herbalist! We'll teach you all you need to know about the various medicinal herbs and how they may best be used to treat symptoms and improve your overall well-being. Perhaps more importantly, we'll ensure that you know how to use herbs safely and effectively. Herbal medicine involves much more than drinking a few cups of tea and eating leaves . . . so let's get started!

Chapter 1: Herbal Medicine Basics

Herbs have been used for medicinal purposes for tens of thousands of years, and it's only in recent decades that herbalism has come to be known as an "alternative" medicine. However, even though mainstream medicine no longer directly prescribes herbal treatments, many modern medicines utilize elements of plants; additionally, the use of medicinal herbs is beginning to increase, as information spreads about their uses and studies support their benefits.

History of Herbal Medicine

Archaeology suggests that humans have used plants and herbs to treat injuries and illnesses for nigh on 60,000 years. Many of history's greatest cultures—including ancient Egypt, Greece, Rome, and China—prescribed and recorded medicinal herbs.

Although modern medicine has become the dominant force in much of Western society, herbalism continues to flourish in many parts of the world. People are able to grow their own herbs or find them in nature; this ease of access and increased affordability make herbs an easy choice for countries where the cost of health care is too high.

Safety Guidelines for Using Medicinal Herbs

While, in many cases, modern medicine has competed with traditional herbal remedies, scientific developments have also benefited herbalism and its practitioners. Some herbs, though used for medicinal purposes, can actually be harmful and have negative side effects for users. Scientific studies have provided more in-depth and reliable information for herbalists about which plants are safe and proven to be effective, and about which plants can be toxic and should be avoided or treated with caution.

This is one of the most important key concepts that must be understood by all herbalists. The fact that something is all-natural does not mean that it is unquestionably healthy. Poison ivy is "all-natural," as are rhubarb leaves, mistletoe berries, and hemlock—all of which are poisonous and may even prove fatal. Don't blindly trust that any herb in any form is good for you.

Before you use any herbal medicine, you should have a thorough understanding of herbs and their benefits and risks, such as that provided in this book. You should also meet with your doctor; if you are taking any prescription medications, your doctor can advise you about the safety of specific herbs. You need to be careful when mixing herbal medicines with prescriptions. Your doctor can tell you whether it is safe to use herbal remedies while taking your prescription medication, or if you have any other health conditions that may make herbal medicine a safety concern.

Pregnant mothers, breastfeeding women, and children should also be especially cautious with herbal remedies, and it may be best to avoid herbs entirely. Never administer an herbal medicine to your child without speaking to your doctor first.

Be aware that, although herbal medicines have been used for thousands of years, many are still not fully understood. Science has begun to investigate the powers of herbs, and while it has validated many traditional herbal treatments, there is much that is still unknown, and so there may be some risk involved in taking herbal medicines.

Overview of Herbal Medicine

Herbalism is a very vast field, as there are many different herbs that can be used in a variety of ways to treat a whole array of illnesses and injuries. You can even use herbs to balance your mind and your mood and to prevent sickness, much the same way you might eat citrus fruit during cold season.

There are a number of ways you can harness the healing powers of herbs to treat your ills. Tinctures, decoctions, infusions, poultices, baths, capsules, and ointments are all common forms of herbal medicine.

A tincture is made by soaking the desired herb in a mixture of water and alcohol. A very small amount of the resulting liquid is then taken by mouth, either alone or mixed into a drink.

Decoctions are essentially teas made from bark or roots. The herb is boiled in water for a long period of time in order to fully access the active healing properties of the plant and the resulting liquid is then taken by the mouth.

An infusion is essentially tea; to prepare an infusion, you steep herbs in hot water, strain them out, and drink the remaining liquid. While some infusions may not taste quite as nice as regular tea, some are quite similar to the familiar and popular beverage. In fact, some teas that people regularly drink simply for the taste can offer their drinkers health benefits as well!

A poultice is an herb mixture that is applied on the skin, usually used to treat cuts, rashes, or burns. Some poultices involve applying herbs directly to the skin, while others place herbs between layers of cloth.

Baths are precisely what they sound like; some herbs may be added to a hot bath, and the patient then soaks in the warm water for a prescribed amount of time. The hot water vapors alone can be beneficial, but many of the health benefits of the herbs are absorbed through the skin.

Herb capsules are commonly carried in stores as nutritional supplements and may contain many popular and beneficial herbal medicines, such as Echinacea. Capsules are easily swallowed as regular pills, and the herbs are absorbed by the body during digestion.

Preparing an ointment involves a little more effort, but herbal ointments can be applied to the skin in much the same way as medicinal ointments that you might find in the store. To make an ointment, you mix herbs with either oil or fat, and then follow a recipe to cook the mixture.

Which form you use varies greatly, depending on both the nature of the illness or injury and the type of herb you wish to use. Make sure you choose the right form of medicine for each individual treatment.

Chapter 2: Herbal Antibiotics and Antivirals

While the common cold may be *common*, its occurrence is nonetheless miserable. A runny nose, sore throat, persistent cough, and muscle aches may linger for weeks at a time, and while a cold rarely keeps you from work or school, it will infest everything in your life with germy misery.

Colds and other common viral or bacterial infections ail many people, and oftentimes, there is little that doctors can do. The body must fight off viruses on its own, and many bacteria are developing immunities to antibiotics.

However, this is no cause for despair; there are a number of herbs that can be used to treat the symptoms of bacterial and viral infections and to aid and strengthen the body's immune system.

Study the list of herbs below to determine which herbal remedies will best treat your symptoms.

Cayenne Pepper

Cayenne pepper can help individuals with digestive problems or poor circulation. Cayenne can be used to help clear the sinuses and induce sweating, which may help to reduce fevers. As a result, it can also be a useful herbal treatment for the cold or flu.

To relieve sinus congestion and treat a head cold, add a dash or two of dried cayenne pepper to a hot tea. You could also create a gargle by adding roughly half a teaspoon of dried cayenne pepper and two Tablespoons of salt to two cups of boiling water. Gargling this mixture can relieve sore throat and congestion, which are symptoms of many common illnesses.

It's important to be careful when preparing and treating illness with cayenne pepper. Some individuals are particularly sensitive, so you should start with small doses in case the cayenne creates a burning sensation in your mouth, throat, or stomach. Avoid getting cayenne pepper in your eyes, and don't take cayenne pepper regularly. Also, do not use cayenne pepper if you have an extremely high fever or an irregularly fast heart rate.

Chamomile

Chamomile is most commonly known as a tasty tea, but this popular beverage also packs in a host of medical benefits. Chamomile is known for its calming effects and its ability to ease nausea, indigestion, and the symptoms of irritable bowel syndrome. However, chamomile has also demonstrated some antibiotic abilities and can help users fight off infection.

In addition to its tea form, chamomile may also be taken as a tincture or may be applied to skin problems as a poultice or herbal bath. Although some people may experience an allergic reaction to chamomile, it is an extremely safe herb for most and very few people experience any negative side effects.

Echinacea

Echinacea is one of the most valued and trusted herbal remedies for colds, flus, and other common illnesses or infections. Apart from a potential allergic reaction, no negative side effects of Echinacea are known, no matter the dosage size or frequency. Because of the herb's safety, frequent large doses are recommended at the onset of any illness.

Echinacea is regularly found in capsules, but it may also be taken in teas or tinctures. You don't need to be concerned about overdosing, and instead can focus on supplying your system with plenty of this herb, which improves immune function and helps the body fight off disease.

Eucalyptus

Eucalyptus is another popular herbal remedy that can be found in many commercial stores. Eucalyptus is often used to treat colds and other common illnesses, as it helps to reduce cough and congestion while soothing sore throats. The plant also serves as an antibiotic, and so may be used to kill germs in the mouth or to treat wounds on the skin.

Eucalyptus may be prepared in a tea or tincture, but it's also easy to find commercial products containing eucalyptus. Many stores carry toothpastes, cough drops, syrups, mouthwashes, and chest rubs that use eucalyptus, and you may find that it's more convenient to simply purchase these products rather than to prepare your own remedy.

Don't ingest eucalyptus oil unless it's prepared in a commercial product that is intended to be taken orally. Otherwise, stick to applying eucalyptus to the skin. When used topically, eucalyptus is quite safe. However, pregnant women should avoid using eucalyptus, and remember to speak with your doctor before taking any herbal medicine—especially if you have a preexisting condition.

Feverfew

Feverfew is a plant that is primarily used to treat migraines, but it can also reduce menstrual cramps and lower fevers. You may take feverfew in a capsule, infusion, or tincture, or you may even choose to simply eat dried feverfew leaves.

Feverfew should not be used during pregnancy. Potential side effects of its use include nausea and irritation in the mouth, usually a result of chewing the dried leaves. If this occurs, simply switch to taking your dose in capsules or a tincture instead.

Garlic

While the supposed vampire-warding abilities of garlic have been known for centuries, the plant's numerous health benefits have also been common knowledge. Garlic functions as an antibiotic, antifungal, and antiviral, and the herb is also known to benefit blood pressure and the immune system. Some studies even suggest that garlic may reduce the risk of certain cancers.

As you can imagine, garlic is also one of the easiest herbs to ingest. Rather than preparing a special infusion or purchasing separate capsules, you can simply include garlic in your regular meals. (Just remember your breath mints!) However, you can also take garlic in capsules, tinctures, or infusions.

Garlic is usually quite safe, but some individuals may experience an allergic reaction, heartburn, or nausea. You should also be aware that garlic seems to act as a blood thinner, so you should limit your garlic consumption before or after surgery.

Ginger

Ginger helps improve circulation and can be used to treat digestive problems and nausea. For this reason, it may be of particular use to those suffering from the stomach flu, although it is often used by those suffering from indigestion, gas, and arthritis as well.

Ginger is regularly taken in capsules, and the herb is usually quite safe. However, you should avoid taking a large dose of ginger, and don't use ginger if you have a high fever.

Ginseng

One of the most popular herbs, ginseng offers a number of benefits ranging from reduced cholesterol to cured headaches to improved immunity. Ginseng is particularly useful for the elderly, but may also be used by those affected by hypertension, chronic stress, and fatigue. If you find yourself constantly coming down with some new illness, your immune system may be worn down by stress and could benefit from the use of ginseng.

Because this herb is so popular, there are a variety of ways in which you may use it. You can find ginseng in teas, tonics, capsules, and tinctures, and your preferences dictate which is right for you.

While no serious side effects have ever been reported, you should avoid overdosing on ginseng. Some herbalists recommend taking regular doses of ginseng for a week, followed by a week off. By alternating in this way, you can avoid oversaturating your system with ginseng. If you do find yourself experiencing negative side effects after taking ginseng, stop your doses and any side effect should clear up quickly.

Goldenseal

Goldenseal is an extremely popular and effective herbal medicine used to treat bacterial infections, inflammation, and digestive problems. It is usually taken as a tincture or capsule, as its taste is extremely bitter. People suffering from a sore throat may wish to combine goldenseal with myrrh and Echinacea in a gargle.

Overall, goldenseal is quite safe and users don't experience any negative side effects. However, it should not be taken by pregnant women. Because goldenseal is so popular, it has been overharvested in recent years, and so you should also avoid regular consumption of the herb and instead opt for other medicinal plants when possible.

Horseradish

As anyone who has ever eaten horseradish can imagine, this herb is fantastic for clearing the sinuses. It is excellent for treating sinus infections, the common cold, and the flu, as it helps ease your breathing and get rid of mucus. It also has some antibiotic qualities and can aid your immune system in fighting off infection more quickly.

While you may choose to use the commercially packaged horseradish that is found in stores, using the fresh root is preferable. It can be grated and mixed with honey or vinegar to create your own horseradish sauce, which is easily spread on crackers or bread.

If you take horseradish to treat congestion, you'll likely notice an annoyingly runny nose in the days following. Although unpleasant, this is actually a good sign, as it means that your body is thinning and removing the mucus rather than allowing it to continue accumulating.

Horseradish is generally safe, but you should avoid overly large doses. If you experience any nausea, vomiting, or headaches, there's likely no reason to be concerned, but cease taking doses of horseradish.

Licorice

The licorice plant was frequently used to flavor candy, but its taste is not its only benefit. Licorice can be used to treat a number of different ailments. It functions as an anti-inflammatory and an antiviral, and may also be used to treat cold sores and ease coughing.

You may take licorice through a tincture, capsule, or syrup. Small amounts may be taken regularly when mixed with other herbs, either to flavor or balance herbal medicines. Larger amounts may be taken to treat a particular illness, such as the cold, an irritable bowel episode, or a cold sore.

While licorice is generally free from side effects, it may raise the user's blood pressure and so should be avoided by those with hypertension. Pregnant women should also be extra careful to avoid licorice, and you should generally avoid extremely large doses or long-term use of licorice.

Marshmallow

(No, not that kind.)

The mallow family of plants can be used to treat a number of common ills, and have proved particularly useful in curing bladder infections. Mallow is generally prepared by chopping and drying the roots to create infusions or tinctures. Teas are the preparation of choice for treating bladder infections, and the mallow root may be combined with other antimicrobial herbs, such as thyme or Oregon grape.

There are no known side effects of the marshmallow plant, so it's safe to ingest large amounts of the herb in order to treat infections.

Myrrh

Myrrh is both an anti-inflammatory and antimicrobial, meaning that it treats both the symptoms and causes of many bacterial illnesses. Individuals who are affected by bronchitis, tonsillitis, sore throat, and colds may find healing in myrrh treatments.

While myrrh does not taste particularly nice, it can be mixed with water and other herbs to create a gargle that will treat the mouth and throat directly.

Myrrh is generally safe in small doses, but never take a dose exceeding two grams. Also, be careful using myrrh if you have a fever, and as always, be wary if you have any other health conditions. Pregnant women, those with diabetes or heart issues, and anybody who has an upcoming surgery or recently came out of a surgery should speak to a doctor before taking herbal medicine.

Oregon Grape

Oregon grape is a plant that is often used to treat infections and to improve liver function. It's highly effective as an antibiotic or antiviral, and so is useful to those suffering from the cold, flu, or other common infection.

Oregon grape may be taken in a tea, capsules, or a tincture, but should be combined with other herbs in order to drown out the extremely bitter taste of the plant.

While there are no known side effects of the Oregon grape, you should avoid long-term use, and pregnant women should steer clear of this herbal remedy.

Thyme

Thyme is an herb commonly found in the kitchen, but its uses extend far beyond seasoning food. Thyme improves respiratory function and can treat coughs, including those associated with the common cold and bronchitis.

Rather than using thyme leaves, you might purchase the essential oil, which can be combined with olive oil and rubbed into your chest to relieve coughing. Thyme can also be administered through a tincture, tea, or water vapors.

While there are very few side effects associated with thyme, large doses may cause nausea. Also, if you are using thyme essential oil, know that you should never use it in its pure form. Thyme essential oil is extremely strong and should always be diluted with another substance before application.

Chapter 3: Herbal Medicine for Injuries

Herbal remedies aren't solely reserved for illnesses and infections, but can also be used to treat injuries.

Read through the list of herbs below to find out what herbs are used for what types of injuries.

Aloe Vera

Anyone who's ever experienced a particularly bad sunburn is sure to be familiar with the healing powers of aloe vera. Aloe can be used to treat any number of skin conditions, from burns to rashes to dandruff or acne. Many studies have supported the benefits of aloe vera, and one study even discovered aloe's success in treating leg ulcers.

Aloe vera products are extremely accessible, and it's easy to find aloe vera gel or cream in many stores. If you prefer to make your own herbal remedies, however, you can also harvest the leaves of the aloe vera plant, scrape out the leaves to collect the pulp, and mash it all together to create a gel that can be applied to the skin.

While there are no known side effects of external aloe vera use, there are some risks to ingesting aloe vera. In spite of claims that aloe vera can be used to treat digestive troubles, you may be wiser to stick to external use of aloe only.

Black Cohosh

The black cohosh plant functions as an anti-inflammatory and can be used to treat aches of any sort, whether they're the result of an injury or a condition such as arthritis or menstruation.

Black cohosh remedies use the root of the plant and are regularly administered through a tincture or capsule. When taking black cohosh, be careful to avoid an overdose, as this may result in side effects such as dizziness, headache, diarrhea, vomiting, and tremors.

While a very small percentage of people experience side effects are regular use of black cohosh, the plant should be safe for all except for pregnant women and individuals with heart conditions—both of whom should avoid taking black cohosh.

Calendula

The flowers and leaves of calendula can be useful in treating wounds and skin conditions. Calendula may be prepared in a lotion or salve, which can then be applied directly to the skin, or as a mouthwash or gargle, which is used to treat injuries in the mouth or throat.

There are no known side effects of calendula, but you should take some precautions when applying it to certain types of wounds. Never use calendula salve or lotion, which is fat-based, on an oozing wound; you might instead choose to apply calendula tea, and then allow the area to dry completely before applying again. Also, don't use calendula on freshly stitched injuries. Wait until the stitches have been removed.

Comfrey

Comfrey is an herb that is highly valuable in treating exterior injuries or skin conditions, but should never be ingested, as it may lead to liver damage when taken internally. Instead, the roots of the comfrey plant can be used to prepare lotions, teas, poultices, or salves for external injuries.

When selecting which form of medicine to make, be aware that the comfrey plant tends to mold. Poultices and teas are therefore easier to make and use. A rag soaked in comfrey tea or a comfrey poultice may be applied directly to burns or lacerations to speed up healing.

Comfrey is completely safe for topical use, but do *not* use it internally.

Oats

Oats are not only a healthy and tasty snack, but are a treat for your skin as well. Many oatmeal soap products are sold commercially, as oats are known to benefit dry, flaky skin and to treat skin rashes. Whether you want to use oats for the internal benefits, such as lowered cholesterol, or the external benefits for your skin, oats are a valuable herbal medicine.

For internal use, the simplest method is to simply prepare and eat oatmeal. However, teas and tinctures can also be made from oats if you prefer to reap the benefits of oats this way. To treat your skin, you can prepare an oat bath by filling a cloth with oats and allowing it to soak in your hot bath.

While there are no real side effects of oats, some people may experience an allergic reaction or digestive troubles resulting from the overconsumption of oats. If you are bothered by either of these, cease any oat treatments.

Slippery Elm

Slippery Elm is an anti-inflammatory that can be used to reduce swelling and cure injured tissue.

The bark of the slippery elm tree may be used to prepare a decoction, a tea made by extended soaking. However, another common preparation of slippery elm bark is to create a powder, which may then be added to common food items and ingested. Powdered slippery elm bark may be added to anything, ranging from juice to smoothies to oatmeal.

Slippery Elm has no known side effects and is generally considered safe for all individuals.

St. John's Wort

St. John's wort is a plant that has a number of uses, from reducing muscle tension to treating depression and anxiety. Strains, sprains, and cramps may all be treated with St. John's wort.

For external use, you can rub the oil of St. John's wort directly on the skin of troubled areas. For internal consumption, whether for physical injuries or mental illnesses, you can prepare teas and tinctures using St. John's wort, which can then be taken regularly.

For the most part, there are no side effects of St. John's wort. However, a few rare individuals have experienced extreme sensitivity to the sun after extended use of the plant. Although this is rare, you may wish to avoid using St. John's wort for a long period of time in order to minimize the already-small risk of this side effect.

Willow

The bark of the willow tree is frequently used as an herbal remedy for pain and swelling. Willow bark may be used to treat headaches, muscle cramps, body aches, and even tendonitis.

Willow bark is often dried to create teas or tinctures, or it may powdered and encapsulated. While you can take fairly regular doses of willow bark, avoid overdosing and long-term use. As always, be sure to speak with your doctor before beginning any herbal remedy.

Willow bark shares some similarities with aspirin, and so children under the age of 16 should not take it. Additionally, anyone who is sensitive to aspirin should likely avoid willow bark in order to prevent any negative side effects, which may include nausea, headache, vomiting, and ulcers. It's also important to avoid overdoses of willow bark, as this too can lead to the development of negative side effects.

Yarrow

Yarrow is an herb that has been used for centuries to stop bleeding and accelerate the healing of cuts and bruises. Some even suggest that yarrow may be useful in cleaning the wounds that it helps to heal. Yarrow may also be taken internally to regulate a woman's menstrual cycle, minimizing painful cramps and reducing abnormally heavy flows or even increasing irregular flows.

In addition to yarrow's abilities to treat injuries and regulate the menstrual cycle, it also serves as a decongestant and can help people recover from the cold or flu. It may also be used to treat gallbladder troubles, preventing the formation of gallstones and regulating the flow of bile.

Yarrow may be prepared in a number of ways, and can be found as a tea, tincture, capsule, or bath. Ingestion of yarrow, as in a tea, tincture, or capsule, is used to treat internal issues, such as those relating to menstruation, infection, or gallbladder function. To treat external injuries, soak a cloth in an infusion of yarrow and apply it directly to the wounded area.

Some people may discover that they are sensitive to yarrow, and its use may result in headaches or nausea. If this is the case, stop use of yarrow. However, most people experience no side effects and are able to use yarrow without any discomfort or concerns.

Chapter 4: Herbal Remedies

Even if you aren't currently suffering from any illnesses or injuries, herbal medicine can still benefit your mind and body.

Check out these herbs that may serve a number of purposes, from reducing blood pressure, to improving circulation, to stimulating memory.

Burdock

The plants and roots of the burdock plant serve a number of purposes as an herbal medicine. They can be used to improve liver function, improve digestion, treat skin disorders such as acne, and cleanse the body of impurities and toxins.

Burdock can be used in a number of forms, including teas, tinctures, and capsules. You can even eat the burdock root! It's a common food item in some Asian cultures.

Pregnant women and individuals suffering from ulcers or IBS should avoid burdock. While the plant generally has no side effects, it may occasionally cause some stomach upset, which can be particularly troublesome for those who are already suffering from digestive troubles.

Cilantro

Cilantro is commonly used for flavoring food, but this tasty herb also has medicinal purposes. Cilantro is a powerful cleansing agent, helping to purify the body by removing toxic chemicals. Cilantro may also help to aid in cardiovascular health and to reduce anxiety. With all of these health benefits, cilantro is a great and convenient herb to slip into your diet!

Obviously, the easiest way to reap the benefits of cilantro is to use it as seasoning for your food. Generously sprinkle fresh or dried leaves over your meals, and voila!

Cilantro is quite safe, and is regularly consumed by the majority of the population without any concerns or side effects.

Cinnamon

Cinnamon is easily found in nearly every kitchen, and this fragrant spice is not only great for seasoning food and beverages, but also packs in a number of health benefits. Cinnamon may be used to treat arthritis, headaches, and high cholesterol, all while improving digestion.

One of the perks of cinnamon is its ease of use. Simply sprinkle some powdered cinnamon on your meals or in your drinks, and you're good to go! You can also soak a stick of cinnamon in a cup of hot tea, or even purchase cinnamon capsules from certain health stores for easy, measured dosages.

Cinnamon is usually quite safe, but you should avoid taking large amounts, as this can lead to liver or kidney damage. Also, be wary if you're pregnant or taking any blood thinning medications. Some types of cinnamon may function as blood thinners, and so you don't want to combine cinnamon with certain other medications.

Dong Quai

Dong quai, otherwise known as Angelica, is a common herbal treatment for menstrual problems, including cramping, PMS, and irregular cycles. Dong quai functions as a general anti-inflammatory and muscle relaxer, but it has proven to be particularly effective for the uterus. Some people may also use it to treat hypertension or allergies.

Dong quai is frequently taken by mouth, but it may also be applied to the skin in a cream. Dong quai is generally quite safe, but you should avoid long-term use. Very rarely, people experience an increased sensitivity to sunlight after taking dong quai, so beware about sun exposure while taking this herb.

You should also avoid using dong quai if you are on any medication that affects the blood, as the two can interact. As always, speak to your doctor before using any new herbal remedy.

Evening Primrose

Evening primrose can function as a muscle relaxant, helping to relieve cramping and reduce muscle pain, and also serves to ease a range of digestive troubles. The plant can also be used to soothe skin problems, such as rashes or stings.

You can find evening primrose oil in health stores, or you can use the dried plant to make teas or tinctures. To treat skin injuries, create an evening primrose poultice and place it over the affected area.

Evening primrose is usually quite safe, but be careful not to exceed the recommended dosage, and individuals who have epilepsy or are prone to seizures should avoid evening primrose on the whole.

Ginkgo

Ginkgo is a very popular herbal remedy that is used to improve circulation and reduce inflammation. By improving circulation to the brain and heart, ginkgo may also benefit mental function and treat some heart conditions. Some believe that ginkgo can even reduce memory loss and treat depression.

You can find ginkgo remedies in a number of forms, including teas, tinctures, and capsules. However, purchasing standardized ginkgo capsules may be the best way to experience noticeable results without risking uncomfortable side effects, including headaches, nausea, and vomiting.

Gingko is generally safe when following recommended doses. However, be sure to talk to your doctor before taking gingko; this is especially important if you have had or are prone to a stroke.

Lavender

The pleasant scent and calming abilities of lavender have made it a staple for soaps, deodorants, and air fresheners. However, you can also take lavender in other forms and more directly receive its benefits. Lavender's calming effects reduce anxiety and relieve tension, helping to cure insomnia and treat headaches. It may even help with digestive, skin, menstrual, and respiratory problems!

Lavender may be taken internally or externally. The dried herb may be added to food, but perhaps the most popular method of taking lavender is aromatherapy, or inhaling the scent. You can find lotions, oils, perfumes, and soaps that are made using lavender. Lavender products may be applied directly to the skin, particularly around problem areas such as rashes or acne. You may also add lavender to warm bath water.

Lavender is generally safe, although ingesting large quantities of it may have potentially harmful side effects. Some people also have a negative reaction to lavender products on their skin. To avoid this, limit your oral consumption of lavender, and if you experience any rashes or irritation after applying lavender products, reduce or cease your lavender usage.

Lemon Balm

Lemon balm is a plant that gives off a lovely lemony scent, but it also offers a host of medicinal benefits. Lemon balm helps to relieve tension and anxiety, treating headaches, depression, and tiredness. It also helps to cure digestive problems, may lower blood pressure, and seems to be effective for treating the herpes virus. Some people even use it to treat Alzheimer's and ADHD.

Lemon balm may be prepared as a tincture or a tea, or it may be added to certain foods. Lemon balm may also be inhaled as aromatherapy.

While this herb is generally safe, you should use caution, particularly when ingesting it. Don't use more than the recommended dosage, and don't take lemon balm for an extended period of time. Potential side effects of consuming lemon balm include nausea, vomiting, and dizziness. Topical usage of lemon balm should be quite safe, although a very few people have reported skin irritation.

Peppermint

Peppermint is a familiar herb that can be used to ease stomach upset, such as indigestion, cramping, gas, and nausea, and to treat skin problems including pain, itching, and inflammation.

Because peppermint is so popular, you can find a number of commercial products that contain it. Toothpastes, mouthwashes, mints, teas, and ointments all may use peppermint. In addition, you can prepare your own remedies using the peppermint plant. Tea is the most preferred form, and you can purchase commercially prepared peppermint tea bags or you may create your own. To treat skin problems, you may also apply diluted peppermint oil directly to the affected area, and the oil will soothe and cool the irritation.

While most people find peppermint to be perfectly safe, some individuals do experience an allergic reaction with side effects including nausea, headache, and rashes. You should also be careful with peppermint if you have GERD, liver or gallbladder problems, or a hernia, as peppermint may worsen some of these conditions. Generally, avoid taking overly large doses of peppermint and only use it when you need to.

Rosemary

Rosemary is another common herb that can be used medicinally. It is often found in hair care products, as rosemary has been found to prevent premature boldness and stimulate hair health and growth. Rosemary is also used to treat headaches and stomach upset.

To use rosemary for your hair's health, you may purchase hair products that already contain rosemary or you may choose to create your own. Rosemary oil can also be diluted and applied directly to the scalp to treat conditions such as dandruff. For internal use, rosemary tea is perhaps the most popular preparation available. You can also add rosemary to food and beverages, as the rosemary leaf and oil may both be used in cooking. Some people also use rosemary for aromatherapy, and the plant can be found in a number of products including soaps and perfumes.

Rosemary is usually quite safe for adults, but you should be careful when ingesting it at medicinal amounts. Never take the undiluted oil by mouth, and measure your doses carefully. If you are pregnant or have a seizure disorder, steer clear of rosemary, as the herb may cause miscarriages or worsen a seizure disorder.

Sage

Sage is an herb that has a long history of use to treat digestive issues, including gas, cramps, diarrhea, heartburn, and bloating. Sage also functions as an antibacterial and may be used to treat bacterial infections, and some people use sage to cure scalp conditions and overly oily hair. There's even some evidence to suggest that sage is successful in treating Alzheimer's disease.

Sage is most often prepared as a tea or tincture, although you may also apply diluted sage oil directly to the skin as a treatment for cold sores. Sage is also a popular herb for cooking, and you can use it to flavor your food. You may also find commercial products that contain sage, such as soaps and fragrances.

The amount of sage usually found in foods is safe for consumption, but be cautious about taking medicinal amounts of sage, particularly for an extended period of time. Some types of sage contain a chemical that can build up in your body and have potentially dangerous side effects, including seizures and internal organ damage. Because of this, it's recommended that pregnant women and individuals with seizure disorders avoid consuming amounts of sage that exceed the portion you would find in food.

Turmeric

This anti-inflammatory herb is commonly found in people's kitchens, but it is also often used to treat tendonitis and arthritis.

Unfortunately, the dried spice that is often used for cooking isn't particularly effective for medicinal purposes (although it certainly doesn't hurt to spice up your food!). Instead, you can find turmeric in standardized capsules.

Turmeric is generally quite safe, although some people experience negative reactions to extended use. If you have been taking turmeric over a long period of time and have irregular nausea, vomiting, or heartburn, stop taking turmeric medicinally. Pregnant women should be sure to check with their doctors before taking turmeric, as should anyone with a gallbladder problem.

Wintergreen

Wintergreen is another medicinal herb that is also commonly used for flavoring in products such as mints, toothpastes, and mouthwashes. In addition to its minty-fresh taste, wintergreen also has qualities that make it useful for reducing pain and swelling, as well as stimulating the digestive system. It is often used to treat headaches, arthritis, menstrual cramps, and digestive problems.

Plenty of commercial products contain wintergreen and may offer some of the herb's medicinal benefits. You may also purchase wintergreen oil, which can be applied topically to painful areas of the body. Wintergreen tea is another popular option.

Wintergreen is generally quite safe, both for topical use and ingestion, but you shouldn't take the oil by mouth. Ingesting wintergreen oil can cause a host of side effects, including nausea and dizziness, and may even result in death.

Valerian

Valerian is particularly useful in relieving anxiety, helping to treat ailments that stem from long-term stress and tension such as insomnia and depression. Valerian also serves as a sedative and muscle relaxer, so it may be useful in relieving cramps and sore, tense muscles.

This herbal remedy may be prepared in a number of ways, including teas, tinctures, capsules, and baths. All of these options are a good method for treating anxiety and insomnia.

Valerian does have some potential side effects that you should be aware of before taking this herb. Some individuals experience headaches or heart palpitations and should stop taking valerian. In some cases, valerian has also been known to have the opposite effect from that intended, stimulating rather than sedating. If this happens to you, begin by reducing your dosage. If this does not fix the problem, however, you may have to find another herbal remedy for your ailment.

Chapter 5: Benefits and Risks of Herbal Medicine

As you can see from the previous three chapters, herbal remedies pack in a myriad of benefits. Plants are able to treat an extremely diverse range of ailments, so whether you sprained your ankle, caught a case of the sniffles, or suffer from arthritis, there's an herbal remedy that's right for you.

Herbs are often quite affordable—particularly when compared to the soaring prices of prescription medications, or even some of their costly over-the-counter counterparts. You can even grow your own herbs at home, so you have a convenient supply of all the medicine you need, instantly at your disposal.

Herbal medicine also offers a number of different options when it comes to dosages. Some people may find that they have a strong preference for teas, while others may prefer to take capsules. When using herbal remedies, you aren't confined to one particular form of medication. If you don't like taking pills, you can try a tincture instead. If you have a hard time forcing down a cup of herbal tea, you might fare better with aromatherapy. You don't have to resign yourself to forcing down unappealing medicines; with herbal remedies, you can find the routine that best works for you.

Another benefit of herbal medicine is that herbs rarely cause side effects. While some people do experience side effects, as you learned in the last few chapters, the likelihood of having a negative reaction to an herb or suffering from negative side effects seems to be much lower than the likelihood of experiencing side effects while taking more mainstream medications.

Herbal remedies are also unlikely to lead to addiction, unlike many prescription medications in the world today. While you may hear of people taking pills recreationally, or becoming addicted to their pain medication, you would likely never hear of a person who was addicted to, say, chamomile or yarrow. When you're treating your illnesses and injuries with herbal medicines, you don't run the same risk of forming an expensive and dangerous addiction.

By choosing herbal remedies, you're also helping to benefit the environment. Herbs grow naturally and are a normally occurring part of their native areas. Mainstream medications, on the other hand, require production and the use of synthetic chemicals. The pharmaceutical industry generates massive amounts of pollution in order to produce its wares, and so by cutting down on the number of mainstream medicines you take and instead choosing herbal remedies, you reduce the amount of pollution that enters the atmosphere.

Also, it's important to note that many prescription medications in use today were originally derived from herbal remedies. Many of the active ingredients in these drugs are found in the plants that are used to treat similar ailments, supporting the idea that herbal medicine is effective and really works.

However, herbal medicine is not without its disadvantages. As you've noticed throughout this book, there are potential side effects and concerns about overdosing that accompany the practice of herbal medicine. It's still important to take care and speak to a trustworthy doctor before using any herbal remedies. The fact that they are derived from plants does not mean that they are unquestionably safe. Remember that herbal medicines are *medicine*, after all, and so they should be treated with caution and wisdom.

You should also remember that you can't rely on herbal medicine for everything. Doctors, hospitals, and mainstream medications certainly have their purposes. While herbs can be used to treat a vast array of ailments, they can't cure everything. Don't think that your herbal remedies are the ultimate answer to health and well-being.

Another disadvantage of herbal remedies is the uncertainty associated with their use. While herbalism has been practiced for thousands of years, only recently have scientists begun to investigate the properties of plants. We still don't have confirmed evidence on the effects—both good and bad—of many herbal remedies. As a result, there is always some risk involved when taking herbal medicines.

There are some things you can do to help minimize this risk, however. Always be extra careful of overdoses, poisoning, and interaction with other drugs, simply because we don't always know enough to ensure that something is safe. Take precautions to ensure that you don't approach the line of danger. *Always, always, always* speak to your doctor before taking any herbal medicine in case it may interact with a drug you're taking or may not be safe for someone in your circumstances.

Finally, herbal remedies are also largely unregulated, so there's no way to guarantee that you're receiving high-quality products. This can also make it difficult to determine doses and to make sure that your remedies are fully effective.

In spite of these disadvantages, herbal remedies still offer a wealth of benefits to wise and careful users. As long as you are fully aware of the risks involved and take every action to prevent any damage, herbal remedies should be a perfectly safe, affordable, and effective way to take care of your mind and body.

Conclusion

Thank you again for downloading this book!

I hope this book was able to help you learn about herbal medicine and how to use it effectively and safely. Herbs are an affordable way to treat a whole host of illnesses, and when you use them wisely, they can be a wonderful, natural way for you to care for your body and mind.

The next step is to put your knowledge to use. You can use herbs to improve your immune system, better your circulation, and relieve stress and anxiety, and next time you're feeling sick, you'll know exactly what to do!

Finally, if you enjoyed this book, please take the time to share your thoughts and post a review on Amazon. It'd be greatly appreciated!

Thank you and good luck!

www.ingramcontent.com/pod-product-compliance
Lightning Source LLC
Chambersburg PA
CBHW070256290526
45789CB00004B/1874